DANNY AND THE iCE CREAM

WEALTH LESSONS FOR KIDS:
THE iMPORTANCE OF COUNTING YOUR MONEY

WRITTEN BY
DANNY RANDAZZO

iLLUSTRATED BY
TAMi BOYCE

DannyRandazzo.com Publishing
Charleston, SC

THIS BOOK IS DEDICATED TO MY WIFE, CAITLIN

FOR HER UNCONDITIONAL SUPPORT OF MY VISION AND PASSION FOR FINANCIAL FREEDOM.

"Ahhhh! Grgle. Giggle Snrfle. Sniggle," said Danny as a sunbeam came through his window and began to fill his room with radiant morning sunlight. "I guess it's time to get up!"

"And streeeeeetch!"

Danny always wakes himself up with a great big yawn and a stretch in the morning before heading over to his favorite spot in the room: his locker! That's where Danny keeps his wallet.

EVERY SINGLE DAY, right after his morning stretch, Danny heads over to his locker to count the money in his wallet.

"One, two, three, four, five, ten," he counts. "Ten dollars! Same as last night!"

Danny is pleased to know that nothing happened to his money while he was sleeping.

"Today is going to be a great day!"

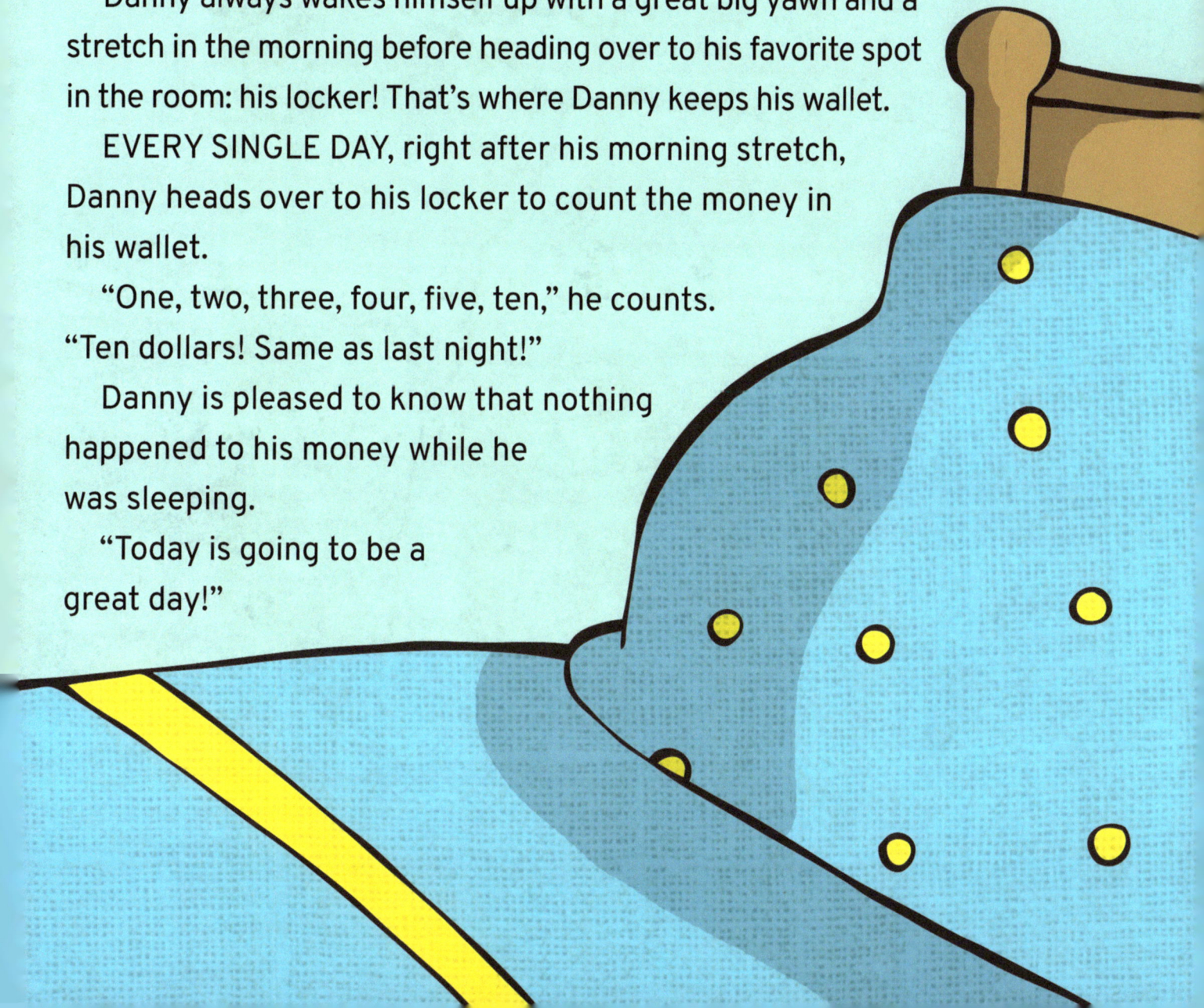

Danny puts his wallet back in his locker with a satisfied smile and heads to the kitchen for breakfast.

"What's up, little brother?" asks Danny's big brother, Joel.

"Whatcha doing?" asks Danny's younger sister, Pippa.

"Oh, you know," answers Danny.

Every day they ask the same questions, and every day they sit down together for a bowl of cereal made a special way by their mother.

"Don't forget to put the bananas in the bottom of my bowl!"

Danny knows his mother never forgets, but he still likes to remind her.

"It's a beautiful summer day outside," says Mom, after pouring milk on three bowls of cereal. " What are you going to do today?

"Let's play hockey in the driveway!" yells Joel.

"I'll be the goalie!" yells Pippa.

And after breakfast, that's exactly what they do. Danny and Joel take shots at the goal while Pippa does a great job defending it. It's really fun, but it's a hot game on a hot day.

"Whew! I'm getting hot," says Pippa, as she wipes her forehead and notices the sun high up in the sky.

"We've been playing a long time," says Joel. "Maybe we should take a little break."

The three hockey players decide to sit down under a shady tree, but it's so hot outside that they hardly cool down at all.

"What's that noise?" wonders Danny.

"What noise?" ask Joel and Pippa together.

But Danny is sure he hears something. It's a faint sound of music that's getting louder and louder and louder.

"I know! I know!" yells Pippa.

But before Pippa can say, Joel chimes in. And he's REALLY loud.

"IT'S THE ICE CREAM TRUCK!!!" he yells.

"I sure wish we could get some ice cream," says Pippa, wiping her forehead again. "But Mom is at work and says we shouldn't bother her unless it's an emergency."

Both Pippa and Joel wonder why Danny hasn't said anything. Danny LOVES ice cream!

Then they look at their brother. Danny is smiling ear to ear!

"Why do you look so happy when we can't get ice cream on this hot day?" asks Joel.

"Oh yes we can," Danny smiles. "I have enough money to buy us some."

And with that, Danny is off like a flash, sprinting to his bedroom to get three dollars for three ice creams—one for each of them.

MENU

SUPERMAN ICE CREAM CUP	$1
FIRECRACKER ICE POP	$0.75
PUSH UP	$0.75
ICE CREAM SANDWICH	$1
FUDGE POP	$0.75

Pippa and Joel wave their arms excitedly as the ice cream truck approaches. The truck slows down and stops.

"Hey, kids! What'll you have?" asks PJ, the ice cream man. He has been here before, and he is wearing a big smile because he knows his customers LOVE ice cream.

"I will please have an ice cream sandwich," says Pippa.

"I will have the firecracker ice pop, please," says Joel.

"GET ME THE SUPERMAN ICE CREAM CUP, PLEASE!!!" Danny yells as he comes out the door.

PJ hands out the treats. "That will be $2.75," he says.

Danny scans the price poster in the truck to make sure PJ did his math right. The ice creams add up to $2.75.

"Here you go," says Danny proudly, as he hands three one-dollar bills to PJ.

"And here YOU go," says PJ as he hands Danny one quarter in change.

"A quarter," thinks Danny. "That's 25 cents. Yup! That's the right change!"

 # MENU

SUPERMAN ICE CREAM CUP $1

FIRECRACKER ICE POP $0.75

PUSH UP $0.75

ICE CREAM SANDWICH $1

FUDGE POP $0.75

After Mom comes home later in the day, Danny is thinking about the ten dollars he had this morning.

"Now I only have $7.25 left," he says to himself.

And then Danny gets a great idea.

"Mom?"

"What, honey?"

"I was wondering. Do you have any jobs for me? Jobs you would pay me to do?"

"Sure!" says Mom. "If you vacuum the car, I'll pay you five dollars!"

"SOLD!" says Danny as he heads for the garage.

Danny is good at vacuuming, and he knows it's important to do your best work when someone hires you for a job.

"Wow! The car looks great!" says Mom, inspecting Danny's work.

"Here's your five dollars, Danny. Thank you! You really are a big help."

"If you want, I'll pay you to weed the vegetable garden tomorrow for SIX dollars," adds Mom.

"SOLD!" says Danny as he counts the money Mom has given him. "One, two, three, four, five!"

As the sun sets on another day, Danny thinks about all the things that happened, including making $5.00 for vacuuming the car.

"I spent $2.75, and then I made five dollars," he says to himself. "And I did two nice things for my family!" he realizes. "I used my money to buy ice cream for Joel and Pippa, and I helped my mom."

"That's a pretty good day!"

Danny flosses and brushes his teeth and then does what he does EVERY SINGLE NIGHT. He counts his money and then puts it in his wallet.

"One, two, SEVEN!" he says, counting the money already in his wallet. "Plus the quarter. Plus the $5.00 from Mom."

"$7.00 plus $5.25 equals $12.25."

"Wow! I have more money tonight than I had this morning," Danny grins. "That's a win in my book!"

"Grllah, grgle grgle!" Danny yawns and stretches again, puts his $12.25 in his wallet, puts his wallet in his locker, and crawls into bed.

Danny drifts off to sleep knowing two important things.

1. You can do good things with your money and still make money.
2. You can get paid for helping people.

THE END

THREE WAYS TO PRACTICE, NOW THAT YOU FINISHED:

1. Spend time counting money at home so kids can add, subtract and make change.

2. Let kids use money to buy a toy or food so they learn how money is exchanged for items of value (Don't use credit all the time!).

3. Ask kids what they would do with $1, $10, or $100 and have them explain why.

ABOUT THE AUTHOR

DANNY RANDAZZO lost his entire net worth at the age of five, an event that taught him to be responsible for his own money no matter what. Following that experience, he earned money by starting small neighborhood businesses and working hard. He became a millionaire before he turned thirty years old using the lessons he learned throughout his life. Today, Danny and his wife Caitlin enjoy taking walks with their dog George and traveling the world. They are real estate entrepreneurs with multiple streams of income. You can learn more about financial freedom and what they do by going to www.DannyRandazzo.com. You can find Danny speaking at national real estate conferences, hosting a real estate meet up, and volunteering with The First Tee, an organization that teaches kids about life through the game of golf.

www.ingramcontent.com/pod-product-compliance
Lightning Source LLC
Chambersburg PA
CBHW041242040426
42445CB00004B/119